SIRENS *of* CHROME

THE ENDURING ALLURE OF AUTO SHOW MODELS

MOMENTUM BOOKS

Published by Momentum Books, L.L.C.

2145 Crooks Road, Suite 208
Troy, Michigan 48084
www.momentumbooks.com
Printed in Canada

ISBN-13: 978-1-879094-84-0
LCCN: 2008935995

Sirens *of* Chrome

THE ENDURING ALLURE OF AUTO SHOW MODELS

MARGERY KREVSKY

INTRODUCTION

"Fair melody! Kind siren! I've no choice."
— FROM *ENDYMION* BY JOHN KEATS, A POEM ABOUT THE PAIRING OF MORTAL AND IMMORTAL (1818).

SIX WOMEN IN DIAPHANOUS DRESSES fan out across a stage swirling yards upon yards of bronze silk over and around a four-wheeled object. Suddenly the cloth drops and a new vehicle rolls out to meet a room full of journalists. Couture "Sirens" with deliberate steps dance in ecstasy to the birthing of a new vehicle.

Think it sounds like a scene from decades past? Think again. This was the reveal of the Buick Enclave sport utility vehicle at the 2006 North American International Auto Show in Detroit. Had the Buick PR executives traveled to ancient Greece to recruit mythological goddesses, they could find no finer talent to weave a spell of enchantment. Within hours, word of the Enclave's debut spread around the world.

Silvery wings, slippery tails, and seductive serenades are synonymous with selling cars. For more than 100 years, automakers have painted posters, erected statues, cast hood ornaments, and commissioned male and female models to mesmerize car buyers with beauty and allure.

The reason is obvious: Sex sells. Just ask any model who's stood before a sea of bedazzled onlookers and fielded the hackneyed question: "Do you come with the car?"

Mythology was a perfect choice for early automotive marketers looking for symbols to relate to their industry. Studying Latin or Greek today is a rarity, but in the early 1900s, it was a staple of the American education system. Schoolchildren grew up on mythological images of Mercury/Hermes—the god of speed—and "Sirens," with their power to lure mortals to their islands through their irresistible song.

Automakers began to employ Sirens to entice mere mortals to worship autos for their speed, looks, and promise of personal freedom and mobility. Their "island" became an exhibit space designed to showcase a vehicle's merits. These ribbon-cutting beauty queens, human hood ornaments, and walking encyclopedias of fuel-economy and towing-capacity specifications sought not to dash ships upon rocks but to entice the purchase of land-worthy ships to sail upon the highways and by-ways of America.

It's been called the fine art of "allure"—and by all indications, the approach works: Industry analysts say two-thirds of adult auto show attendees will buy a new vehicle within a year.

It's no surprise, then, that as auto shows grew, an en-tire industry rose up to supply, wardrobe, and supervise the talent. Consider the throne. A typical turntable in 2007 cost around $50,000 to create and another $10,000 to ship around the country.

But behind the scenes, dressing rooms are filled with tales of trauma inflicted by hours in stiletto pumps, cor-sets, and dangling earrings. Metallic gowns gouge the skin; latex dresses stultify sweat glands.

Some models made a career of alluring patrons; oth-ers used the position as a launch pad for stardom:
- Tim Allen, star of TV's *Home Improvement* and nu-merous movies, was a talent for Cadillac.
- Marilyn Barnett, CEO of Mars Advertising, was a "Dodge Girl" in the 1960s.
- Kathleen DuRoss Ford caught the eye of Ford Motor Co. Chairman Henry Ford II. She married "The Deuce" in 1980.

- Pam Dawber, co-star of *Mork and Mindy*, started as an auto show model before working with Robin Williams.
- Brian "Kato" Kaelin, the famous houseguest of O.J. Simpson, worked as a specialty talent for Nissan.
- Rhonda Walker, a WDIV-TV news anchor in Detroit, was a narrator for Buick.
- Maureen Maher, former CBS news anchor, was a product specialist for Nissan during college.

I came into the business in 1981, hoping to take models out of cleavage-revealing tops, short shorts, and sequined ball gowns. After all, Snow White and Barbie weren't the role models of an increasingly potent corps of women buyers—who now influence 80 percent of all vehicle purchases. We created wardrobes that looked like the brand—from pickup-truck rugged to luxury-se-dan elegant. We even developed a special line of makeup to last under the bright lights.

My company, Productions Plus, has worked with many celebrities at auto shows, from The Dave Brubeck Quartet to Jay Leno. But the consistent stars are our product specialists, who have become the most know-ledgeable in the industry.

I'd like to think I helped the auto show cul-ture evolve out of T&A to a place of professional re-spect. This evolving history—the tale of "allure" if you will—is little known outside of trade magazines or the occasional feature article. *Sirens of Chrome* honors the people who have helped grow and sustain the auto-mobile and its impact on our culture and economy.

— Margery Krevsky, October 2008

 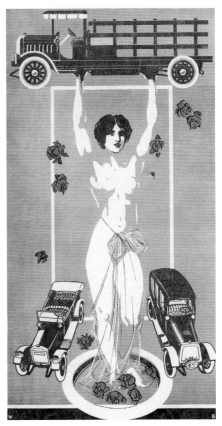

1916

Hermes, god of commerce and speed in Greek mythology (called Mercury by the Romans), drives across the sky with agility in this poster (left). Meantime, a lithograph of a muscular, mythical woman graces the cover of the official program book of the Detroit Auto Show. Such otherworldly symbols would be a part of auto shows for years to come.

1900

Lady of the Flies

AS THIS RARE AND UNUSUAL POSTER DEPICTS, Sirens were not the only creatures with wings visually representing the auto industry. French car company A. Teste Moret & Cie promoted its Voiturette La Mouche ("The Fly") with a classic French Art Deco feeling. The feminine driver is propelled forward by a swarm of harnessed flies.

The import market was developing in tandem with the American auto industry. French vehicles were especially considered fashionable and chic—and had status cachet.

To promote the industry over the next several decades, auto shows in select cities would become annual events. During the next two decades car manufacturers would number in the hundreds, and statues of winged goddesses would fill coliseums and exhibit halls along with four-wheeled, self-propelled carriages.

ILLUSTRATION: National Automotive History Collection at Detroit Public Library

1900

Horseless Housecalls

THE FIRST RECORDED INSTANCE of people being used as models to promote a vehicle is reflected in this rare photograph of a real physician and his family posing in a Stanhope at the Automobile Club of America's first auto show at New York's Madison Square Garden in 1900. Automotive historians suggest doctors were a key market segment at the beginning of the industry, because they needed reliable transportation for making housecalls—and they would have the means to afford it. So instead of hitching up a horse and buggy, the horseless carriage promised speed and the potential for saving lives.

PHOTO: National Automotive History Collection at Detroit Public Library

1900

War of the Wheels

NEW YORK CITY was the backdrop in November 1900 for auto and accessory manufacturers from as far west as St. Louis to display their new contraptions. Crowds attending the Automobile Club of America's show ogled talented acrobats who competed on bicycles and horseless carriages for endurance and agility on a wooden track built around the perimeter of the exposition hall. Cars often won, showing the advancement of these technological wonders. At today's auto shows, you can experience ride simulators, ride with a professional driver, or have an off-road experience in a new vehicle—complete with mud grottoes and waterfalls.

PHOTO: National Automotive History Collection at Detroit Public Library

1906

Siren of Speed

GREETING VISITORS AT THE ENTRANCE OF THE 1906 NEW YORK AUTO SHOW was a lavish 12-foot statue of a heroic female from mythology rising above a show-stopping fountain. Attendees strolled past this *objet d'art* to wander among the approximately 160 cars and chassis displayed by 56 automobile firms. Staged by the Association of Licensed Automobile Manufacturers at Madison Square Garden, this was the beginning of memorable and dramatic displays and exhibits. The "Sirens" or female goddesses were a recurring theme. The show's program book noted: "A heroic female figure representing speed rises with outstretched arms from a fountain with multicolored lights, lush ferns and six gold frogs spouting water in a basin at her feet." Modern-day shows use many of the same elements—lights, water, and dramatic architectural forms—to exhibit automobiles.

PHOTO: National Automotive History Collection at Detroit Public Library

1906

Fashion Drives Function

A PUBLICITY PHOTO BY FORD MOTOR CO. and an automotive accessory ad for sirens (inset) from 1906 are early examples of direct appeals to the female market. However, it wouldn't be for three more years that women would be employed as auto show models. The first documented auto show model was Miss Hazel Jewell. She was called a "product demonstrator" by the *New York Times* in a 1909 article, joining 150 male product demonstrators on the floor of the International Automobile Show at Grand Central Palace in New York.

The photo at right features female models operating a Model N Runabout in fashionable attire—big hats secured with scarves. The siren ad signaled the birth of the accessory market, which created an explosion in automotive patents and ideas for enhancement and comfort. The automobile became a symbol of freedom and personal style, assuring greater contact with the world and emancipating women from household monotony. Still, most affluent women of the day were chauffeured around.

ADVERTISEMENT: National Automotive History Collection at Detroit Public Library
PHOTO: Courtesy of Ford Motor Co.

1908

Winged Wonder

THIS POSTER represents the first of many uses of the Siren symbol to advertise "auto exhibitions," as they were called at the time. In 1908 artist Jean de Paleologue (aka "PAL") designed this color poster of a mythological woman in a transparent gown with wings on her back and feet to herald an import auto salon in New York City. Paleologue —whose bold posters helped sell products from bicycles to skin cream—was selected because there were no artists of the day considered experts in "car art." His rendering served to pique the imaginations of prospective car buyers.

> "Creatures of the air, the Sirens have mastery over space and the summits and the faculty of rising in flight to the heavens. The wings challenge the laws of gravity. The lightness of the feathers implies the speed of a whiplash—sail, glide, vanish, hover."
>
> — *Sirens, Symbols of Seduction* by Meri Lao (Park Street Press, 1998)

PHOTO: National Automotive History Collection at Detroit Public Library

1911

The Spirit of Ecstasy

THE WORLD'S MOST RECOGNIZABLE HOOD ORNAMENT—"The Spirit of Ecstasy"—is the official ornament of Rolls-Royce, created in 1911 by English sculptor Charles Robinson Sykes. Varied automotive scholars credit Eleanor Velaso Thornton as the statue's inspiration. She was a favored Sykes model and courtesan to Lord Montague—a friend of the owners of Rolls-Royce. Thornton died when a German U-boat torpedoed her lover's yacht in the English Channel. But her image lives on. In 2000 Rolls-Royce introduced a retractable "Ecstasy" that automatically slides into a protected well when the engine is shut off, to prevent theft.

Rolls-Royce's Web site comments: "… the spirit of ecstasy, who had selected road travel as her supreme delight and has alighted on the prow of a Rolls-Royce car to revel in the freshness of the air and the musical sound of her fluttering draperies."

PHOTO: Steve Purdy, Shunpiker Productions

1913

Driving Miss Lizzie

FOR MANY PEOPLE, there was a steep learning curve when it came to operating these newfangled pieces of machinery. This 1913 publicity photo from the Ford archives documents a couple learning the fine art of driving a Model T in Detroit's Palmer Park.

Driving was a daunting task, wrote Leon Mandel in his book, *American Cars*. "The driver used both feet and hands, and some coordination between them was required . . . his right limbs he reserved for the far right pedal, a brake that worked on the transmission, and the middle pedal, reverse. The left lever on the quadrant was the ignition control, a spark advance that determined the moment after the intake stroke when the plugs would fire. Once the thing was in motion, it required the use of the left foot and right hand only. ... The Ford took every ounce of your attention ... it would follow every corner, depression, and crack and ridge on the surface, leaping about like a frog on fire."

PHOTO: Courtesy of Ford Motor Company

1916

Changing Times

THE LATE 1800s HAD ANNIE OAKLEY as the adventurous star of Wild West shows. The turn-of-the-century automotive set had Alice Snitzer Burke (opposite page left) and Nell Richardson, suffragists who traveled 10,000 miles across America in a 1916 Saxon—a vehicle directly marketed as a "woman's car." The twosome gained nationwide fame and became darlings of the press. They showed—through necessity—how to change tires, repair engines, replace spark plugs, and deal with rough roads.

After miles on the road and countless repair stops, the two redesigned their wardrobe: Hemlines rose from the top of their shoes to mid-calf and higher because they needed more legroom to operate the floor pedals. Their bustles and corsets bit the dust along with the last vestiges of the Victorian era. Soon more women could become drivers as fashion accommodated car trips and the desire for mobility.

PHOTO: National Automotive History Collection at Detroit Public Library

1919

Silent and Sultry

THE 1919 DETROIT AUTO SHOW PROGRAM BOOK highlighted the silent screen-styled heroine—a sophisticated woman of the world who knows how to drive her future. The chauffeur depicted in many earlier programs had vanished; women could drive themselves. Enter the closed coupe: Gone were the running boards, and the rumble seat debuted. New styling and innovative changes were now part of the industry.

The turbulent Twenties marked a period when sales doubled, variety expanded and cars acquired hard roofs. "Motor Girls" appeared regularly at auto shows as accents to the vehicles. They distributed catalogues for accessories such as headlights, horns, and windshields.

> "Post-war disillusion, the new status of women … the automobile, Prohibition, the sex and confession magazines, and the movies had their parts in bringing about revolution. … Each of them, as an influence, was played upon by all the others; none of them alone could have changed to any great degree the folkways of America; together their force was irresistible."
>
> — Frederick Lewis Allen, former *Atlantic Monthly* and *Harpers'* editor, and author of *Only Yesterday: An Informal History of the 1920s in America*, (Harper Collins, 1997).

PROGRAM: National Automotive History Collection at Detroit Public Library

1922

Drawing a Crowd

CAR BODIES NEVER HAD SUCH CURVES. *Detroit Times* cartoonist Jim Derr penned "A Model to Fit Every Mode"—a direct connection between female auto show models and flashy autos in this January 25, 1922, "Detroit Auto Show Edition" of the newspaper.

CARTOON: National Automotive History Collection at Detroit Public Library

1925

Body Language

AS MAINSTREAM WOMEN HIKED UP THEIR SKIRTS AND PAINTED THEIR FACES for what *Vogue* magazine dictated as feminine style, a new legion of advertisers and marketers hired by the automobile manufacturers penned sensual poetry to their objects of desire—both steel and flesh. A woman with arms open for full-body inspection graces this Fisher Body advertisement with the line, "The user is more continuously conscious of the body of his car …"

PHOTO: Used with permission, GM Media Archives

BODY
FISHER

The user is more continuously conscious of the body of his car than of any other part. It is important, therefore, that he assure himself the comfort, luxury, and enduring satisfaction which is guaranteed by the emblem — Body by Fisher

FISHER BODY CORPORATION, DETROIT
CLEVELAND   WALKERVILLE. ONT.   ST. LOUIS

FISHER BODIES

1927

Damsels of the Dance

PACKARD MOTOR CO. enlisted members of the Marion Morgan Dancers to promote the 1927 model Packard 343 Series Eight. The troupe danced around the United States at auto events and in London in variety shows, specializing in interpretive Greek movement. Here, one member of the troupe performs her interpretation of a 1927 Packard hood ornament. On our back cover, troupe members Elinor, Anoree, Leslie, and Jewel perform a circle ceremony around the convertible coupe.

PHOTO: National Automotive History Collection at Detroit Public Library

1931

Let's Rumble

SILVER SCREEN STARS AND CARS made a glamorous mix. Hollywood used classy and classic cars to define characters and locations. James Cagney and Joan Blondell (foreground), fresh on the publicity trail with a flim-flam 1931 comedy, *Blonde Crazy*, joined Mae Madison in a '31 Ford Model A Deluxe Roadster with an add-on rumble seat.

Sir Hubert Malcolm Rhumble, a prominent carriage designer in the late 1800s in England, designed this reinvented coachman's seat that stuck in the automotive lexicon. The trunklid folded back to form a seat area, sometimes called a "mother-in-law" seat. Certainly, the seat had other passenger advantages.

PHOTO: National Automotive History Collection at Detroit Public Library

1932

As the Wheel Turns

TWO NUDE MEN WITH RIPPLING MUSCLES illustrating "strength and service" are featured on the cover of the Michigan Manufacturer and Financial Record of the Detroit Motor Show in 1932. This painting by F.N. Leyendecker speaks to a growing recognition of auto laborers and the rise of the United Auto Workers union. The painting also is reminiscent of a scene from the 1927 movie, *Metropolis* (directed by Fritz Lang), of a worker valiantly trying to keep pace with a ticking clock, indicating the stress of working on an assembly line.

In 1933, Mexican artist Diego Rivera painted frescoes on the four walls of the main interior courtyard of the Detroit Institute of Arts, representing the power of the automotive industry with depictions of workers, creators, production, raw materials, and the birth of the industry.

VERTICAL FILE: National Automotive History Collection at Detroit Public Library

1934

Luxury Lines

THE APEX OF LUXURY IN VEHICLES was drawing crowds to auto shows around the country. The car was a symbol of glamour, prestige, and fashion. This was not lost on the movie producers and authors of the age. Here, Hazel Forbes, star of *Down to their Last Yacht* and *Bachelor Bait*, lends her bathing suit-clad image to a 1934 Packard Super Eight Convertible Victoria. Such style is reminiscent of author F. Scott Fitzgerald's description of Jay Gatsby's luxury car: "a green leather conservatory … pandered in whispers to the last and greatest of all human dreams."

PHOTO: National Automotive History Collection at Detroit Public Library

1935

Heavenly Floor Plan

IN THIS UNIQUE EXHIBIT MOCK-UP for the 1935 auto show at the Chicago Coliseum, miniature vehicles are specifically placed around information stations. This demonstrated how a pathway was created to guide consumers through the space to a 43-foot-tall mega goddess holding a car. This dramatic symbol combined with two male gods (at the side of the exhibit hall, holding a wheel and an engine) to grab the attention of attendees. At the height of the Depression and labor unrest, visiting an auto show was an opportunity to escape and experience dramatic displays in a beautiful environment.

> "Symbols speak to us in terms of pictures that may be familiar to us in everyday life which represents concepts that move our emotions."
>
> — Manuela Dunn Mascetti, *The Song of Eve: Mythology and Symbols of the Goddess* (Simon & Shuster, 1990).

PHOTO: National Automotive History Collection at Detroit Public Library

1936

Skating on Thin Ice

THE CORD CREATED A SENSATION at the 1936 New York Auto Show. It was in a class by itself with its retractable headlights, front wheel drive, and distinctive "coffin nose" styling. For its publicity campaign, the Cord Corporation enlisted Norwegian figure skater Sonja Henie, who won gold medals in the 1928, 1932, and 1936 Winter Olympics, to pose with the 1936 Cord 810. The car was designed by Gordon M. Buehrig, who later would invent and patent the removable T-top. Mechanical failures and budgetary problems caused Cord to cease production by 1937.

PHOTO: National Automotive History Collection at Detroit Public Library

1936

Glamour Girls

SHOWGIRLS FROM THE 1936 CHICAGO AUTO SHOW smile for a press photo to tout the opening stage extravaganza. These original auto show models worked in fur capes, coats, stoles, and wraps in sable, mink, chinchilla, Persian lamb, and silver fox to the tune of nearly $1 million. Despite hard economic times, viewers sought fashion and entertainment as a tonic for the reality of the times. The buyer demographics were dazzling—those who could afford furs likely had the means to buy new vehicles. Chicago Auto Show attendance, with the help of chorus girls, rose from 125,000 visitors in 1935 to 225,000 in 1939.

PHOTO: Chicago Automobile Trade Association

1938

Glamour School

FIVE MODELS IN GLAMOROUS SATIN GOWNS AND OVERSIZE HATS perform a comedy skit in which a woman declares herself capable of teaching others about the inner workings of a Chevrolet engine at the 1938 Detroit Auto Show. It wasn't until the 1970s that women were granted a microphone and a script to teach patrons about vehicles. For several decades, female models were a beautiful adornment to the motorcars while male counterparts narrated the car's attributes.

PHOTO: Used with permission, GM Media Archives

1938

Selling Safety

MARILYN MESEKE, MISS AMERICA 1938, toured the country, stopping for publicity photos to help announce a driver's education campaign (right) for 5,000 high schools in 33 states sponsored by the Automobile Association of America. The increased size of the vehicle fleet had undesirable side-effects. There were more than 39,500 auto-related deaths in 1937, according to a National Safety Council statistic cited by *Automotive Facts & Figures*. An increased emphasis on safety features helped guard the lives of drivers, passengers, and pedestrians, as shown by a model at the 1939 Chicago Auto Show donning a skeleton suit (inset) to demonstrate the chilling importance of brake safety for an automotive supplier.

PHOTO: National Automotive History Collection at Detroit Public Library
INSET PHOTO: Chicago Automobile Trade Association

1939

There's No Business Like Car Business

"IF IT WAS ENTERTAINING AND DREW CROWDS, it probably appeared at the auto show," wrote Mitchel J. Frumkin and James M. Flammang in their book, *World's Greatest Auto Show* (Krause Publications, 1998). The American show business institution, the Ziegfield Follies, had their counterpart at the auto shows. The cars were the stars and celebrities supported them ... taking second billing. The shows were the talk of the town as in this photo from the 1939 Chicago Auto Show. Full orchestras, dancing chorus girls, crooners, and magicians filled the stage. The costumes and scenery were elaborate, and the production quality spared no expense. The auto show opening event was attended by political leaders, celebrities, and automotive magnates.

PHOTO: National Automotive History Collection at Detroit Public Library

1939

Passing the Torch

FOR ITS 40TH ANNIVERSARY AT THE 1939 NEW YORK AUTO SHOW, the Automobile Manufacturers Association created a wall-sized mural of the Parthenon at the show entrance. Here was a neon outline of Athena, goddess of wisdom and industry, merging with a giant autoworker. This symbolized the power and strength of a growing corps of workers steadily propelling the industry forward—not on wings, but on raw strength and determination. The torch is passed.

PHOTO: National Automotive History Collection at Detroit Public Library

1940

Hoop-De-Do Review

THE DAME FASHION REVIEW OF 1940 included leggy dancers, tuxedoed men, and a "musical mélange" for patrons of the Chicago Auto Show. At one point a vehicle drove through an 18-foot tall hoop skirt. The front curtain is an extraordinary 73 feet high. Performances, according to the authors of *World's Greatest Auto Show,* ran the gamut from opera to jitterbug. Outside the arena, crowds gravitated to nightclubs featuring jazz, minstrel shows, dancing ensembles, and cabarets with a "whirl of girls."

PHOTO: Chicago Automobile Trade Association

1940

Yankee Doodle Divas

A CAST OF PERFORMERS DRESSED IN PATRIOTIC COSTUMES sang a medley of American songs during the twice-daily music review at the Chicago Auto Show in 1940 on the cusp of America's entry into world war. Car dealers later sang the blues when manufacturers ceased auto production between 1942 and 1945, suspending auto shows and advertising campaigns until the war ended. However, when civilian production resumed, it marked the beginning of the Baby Boomer era—a home, a new car, and a family were the focus of many men returning from military service.

PHOTO: Chicago Automobile Trade Association

1942

Holding Down the Fort

PATRIOTIC SOPHISTICATES helped the war effort by posing with military guards at the Fort Wayne induction center in Detroit in their 1942 Ford Super Deluxe—the last series of cars produced until the war ended in late 1945. Automotive plants were taken over by the war effort to produce tanks, planes, armament, and machinery. Men left the assembly lines to "join up," and women replaced them on the job.

Note the license plate: "FM 1942." According to auto historian Michael W.R. Davis, Ford struck a deal for numerous years with the Michigan Secretary of State to put special plates on its vehicles for advertising and media review. FM represents the initials of Ford Motor Co. The vanity plate is born.

PHOTO: Courtesy of Ford Motor Company

1943

Patriotic Dreams

THIS WW II ERA MODEL'S STRIPED DRESS NEXT TO HER BEAU'S UNIFORM in this advertisement conjured visions of Sunday drives to the country and romantic picnics—suggesting that car buying might be a patriotic duty. The phrase "on the beam" at the top of the ad was originally a nautical term that had been adapted by aviators to mean "on the right track." New car styling was on the horizon with integrated bumpers, sleek lines, and ample room in the backseat for young children. Soldiers and war brides would soon make the great surge to suburbia. Suburban migration escalated car culture and eclipsed mass transit.

ADVERTISEMENT: Courtesy of Ford Motor Company

YOU'LL BE "ON THE BEAM"...

There's a *Ford* in your future!

It's a picture that will have to wait. America has an important job to do before your smart, peacetime Ford can be produced. ... But when your new Ford does arrive, you'll be proud of it. For it will be big and roomy—have plenty of "go". Its styling will be youthful, beautiful.

Inside and out, it will be rich appearing—with many refinements. Naturally, it will be thrifty and reliable—as all Ford cars have been for more than 40 years. ... Yes, exciting new fun is in the offing for you. For some day the necessary word will come through. And we'll be ready to start our production plans. Un-

til that time, however, the full Ford resources will continue to be devoted to the needs of final Victory.

FORD MOTOR COMPANY

"THE FORD SHOW". Brilliant singing stars, orchestra and chorus. Every Sunday, NBC network. 2:00 P.M., E.W.T., 1:00 P.M., C.W.T., 12:00 M., M.W.T., 11:00 A.M., P.W.T.

1946

Float On

"MORE AND BETTER THINGS FOR MORE PEOPLE" embellished a chariot GM created for the Golden Jubilee of the Automobile in 1946. Siren models were robed in goddess-inspired gowns and tiaras atop a float resembling a chariot. Each woman triumphantly carried a banner naming her brand. A two-week celebration and parade marked the shift of factories from war machinery back to passenger cars. Six blocks of Woodward Avenue, Detroit's main street, were painted gold—recalling an ancient Roman soldiers' victory march tradition. Car ownership was about to eclipse mass transit. However, the trolley tracks over which these floats passed would still be used for a decade—the last Detroit streetcar rolled to a close in April 1956.

1946

Radiant ... and Radioactive?

MARY GRACE SIMESCU, "Her Automotive Majesty" for the Automotive Jubilee in 1946, waved a wand of neutron-splitting beryllium over a tube of boron, smashing a boron atom and transmitting an electric impulse, which illuminated a spiraling neon symbol of the celebration. While her gesture signified a peacetime use of atomic power, few Americans were yet aware of the dangers of radiation or the potential power it represented. Cutting-edge ideas from power sources to new technology began to be of interest to consumers. Manufacturers invested heavily in research labs, hiring scientists and technicians to create better cars.

PHOTO: National Automotive History Collection at Detroit Public Library

1948

Sirens and Cyclops

MODELS APPEARED AT THE NEW YORK AUTO SHOW IN 1948, encouraging patrons to take a road trip in the Tucker 48 (nicknamed the Tucker Torpedo), built in a 93-acre factory in Chicago. Only 51 vehicles were made in the two-year life of Preston Tucker's undercapitalized, over-promoted firm. The vehicle boasted several unique features, from a front trunk to a "cyclops eye" headlight in the middle of the vehicle that moved when the steering wheel turned. Industry analysts said the owner was far short of automotive experience. He died in 1956, but his legacy endures in a 1988 film by Francis Ford Coppola, *Tucker: The Man and His Dream,* starring Jeff Bridges. Its tagline: "When they tried to buy him, he refused. When they tried to bully him, he resisted. When they tried to break him, he became an American legend."

1950

Excess-orized

THE CADILLAC DEBUTANTE set Chicago Auto Show patrons buzzing in 1950. One of the first concept cars unveiled by GM, its upholstery included 187 Somali leopard pelts, and its hardware was plated in 24-karat gold. The model wore a suit adorned with real leopard collar and cuffs. Visitors gawked at this canary yellow-painted convertible, valued at an extraordinary price of $35,000. Today that cost is priceless as animal protection laws forbid the killing of endangered species. Show cars, concept cars, and vehicles that challenged the imagination were real draws. Concept designers tantalized the public with new innovations, colors, sweeping changes, and fabrications. Car magazines loved these vehicles for their showmanship, and America's love affair with the car intensified.

1953

Fashion Statement

IN APRIL 1953, the Greater New York Automobile Dealers Association enlisted the Hattie Carnegie Salon (a leading couturier of the era) and the "manufacturers of many leading makes of America's finest cars," to provide the latest travel styles for women. These were all paired with show-stopping vehicles, according to the "Easter Parade of Stars Automobile Show" brochure. To be sure, automakers capitalized on style in coming years. Car culture expert Charles L. Stanford quoted the late George Romney, president of American Motors Corp., as saying: "The automobile business has some of the elements of the millinery industry in it, in that you can make a style become the hallmark of modernity."

PROGRAM: National Automotive History Collection at Detroit Public Library

Fashions on Parade

LATEST STYLES FOR TRAVEL

FROM

"EASTER PARADE OF STARS"

AUTOMOBILE SHOW

AND HATTIE CARNEGIE

SALON

1953

Song of the Chevy Siren

MYTHICAL SIRENS WERE KNOWN FOR THEIR VOICES. And customers descended on car dealers in droves after Dinah Shore belted out "See the U.S.A. in Your Chevrolet," the signature piece on her 1950s television show. Shown here at the 1953 Los Angeles Auto Show with then-husband George Montgomery, the celebrity personified the brand and the spirit of the cars. Her weekly TV show, sponsored by Chevrolet, was watched nationally by thousands of consumers … who consumed this song into their psyche.

PHOTO: H.B. Stubbs Companies

1954

Merry Mannequins

SIX MANNEQUINS ON LILY PADS twirled around a 1954 Fire Arrow Coupe concept car—produced by Ghia, an Italian body builder, on a Dodge chassis. Automakers were discovering the mutual benefit of working together on projects. These kinds of partner relationships would increase as the industry demanded more products.

Elaborate turntables created by firms such as H.B. Stubbs and George P. Johnson Companies in metro Detroit became commonplace as a way to showcase all sides of a car to salivating show patrons. Most turntables stand 18 inches off the ground, about kneecap height. This is just high enough for viewers to see a live presenter and low enough to keep the underbody out of view. Exhibit spaces that feature animation and interactivity automatically draw the eyes of show patrons.

PHOTO: National Automotive History Collection at Detroit Public Library

1955

Magical Motorama

GENERAL MOTORS CREATED ITS OWN STAGE SHOW MAGIC with "Here's Looking at You." The show featured a cast of some 20 actors and actresses backed by a big-name band performing six 30-minute shows daily at exhibition halls throughout the U.S. The cars and props traveled in 125 semi-trailers adorned in red, white, and blue graphics created by exhibit builder H.B. Stubbs in suburban Detroit. As a traveling advertisement, the trailers created news stories and media hype and boosted auto show attendance.

PHOTO: National Automotive History Collection at Detroit Public Library

1955

To Catch an Isetta

FRESH ON THE PUBLICITY TRAIL for Alfred Hitchcock's Movie, *To Catch a Thief*, Cary Grant poses in 1955 with a BMW Isetta in Munich, West Germany. The vehicle, only 7.5 feet long and 4.5 feet wide, had a single front entrance and three wheels. Introduced in Italy in 1953, it gained the BMW badge in 1955 when a 250cc four-stroke engine was added. The Isetta appeared in European car shows in 1955 and at the New York Auto Show in 1956. (No, Grant did not come with the car.)

PHOTO: National Automotive History Collection at Detroit Public Library

1955

Bathing Beauties

IN ADDITION TO THE AUTO SHOWS, manufacturers created spectacular auto-focused events like the General Motors Powerama, a $7 million, 26-day showcase of highway and off-road construction vehicles powered by GM diesel engines. When this show was erected on Chicago's lakefront in 1955, heavy equipment dealers and road building companies watched a bevy of bathing beauties splash about in a 4-foot pool mounted inside a Euclid 50-ton LLD truck. *Time* magazine noted GM built a grandstand where 7,000 spectators could watch an hour-long musical titled, "More Power to You." The construction work trucks would be in big demand—one year later, President Dwight D. Eisenhower signed the Federal Aid Highway Act appropriating $25 billion for construction of 40,000 miles of interstate highways over the next 10 years.

PHOTO: Used with permission, GM Archives

1956

Driving the Economy

SHARON RITCHIE—the 18-year-old Miss America from Denver, Colorado—and New York Mayor Robert Wagner cut the ceremonial ribbon for the 1956 New York Auto Show. *Automotive News* found U.S. car and truck sales in America had inched up to 7.8 million in 1955, setting a robust tone for the captains of industry standing behind a simulated car with several steering wheels. Appearing from left to right are: Harold Churchill, president of Studebaker-Packard Corp., Harlow Curtice, president of General Motors, Henry Ford II, president of Ford Motor Co., L.L. Colbert, president of Chrysler, and George Romney, chairman of American Motors. The theme for the show was "America on the Move."

PHOTO: National Automotive History Collection at Detroit Public Library

1956

Ten Speed

TEN DASHING MEN IN STRAW HATS AND STRIPED JACKETS cycled into the State Fair Coliseum in Detroit in the mid 1950s, where they helped cut the ribbon for the Detroit Auto Show and created a buzz around the emerging core of compact cars from Rambler, Studebaker, and Willys. Steering the 10-seater through cars, crowds, and display banners was no small feat for the cyclists. The bike remains on display at The Henry Ford museum in Dearborn, Michigan.

PHOTO: National Automotive History Collection at Detroit Public Library

1957

Fin Fest

A MODEL POSES WITH THE 1957 PONTIAC STAR CHIEF CONVERTIBLE COUPE, replete with tailfins—the iconic symbol of the 1950s when the freedom of mobility overtook America. Between 1947 and 1970, the combined highway expenditures by local, state, and federal governments totaled $249 billion, authorizing ribbons of concrete called "freeways." Now the public could travel almost anywhere in the U.S. in their own dream machine. Dual-car households were becoming a standard in the American lifestyle.

Auto shows now featured 360-degree turntables in their exhibits with male narrators and beautiful girls as an accessory. Suburban malls and convention centers produced their own car shows. The auto show was beginning to become an American tradition, like baseball and apple pie.

PHOTO: Used with permission, GM Media Archives

1958

Racing Stripes

MODELING AGENCIES HELPED AUTOMAKERS create and manage teams of talent for the auto shows, publicity photoshoots, and the rigorous event circuit. Promoting the pure American sports car, Chevrolet marketers in 1958 dressed a model in the same seat upholstery fabric as this Corvette, thereby giving show patrons the pleasure of viewing the car in steel and flesh.

PHOTO: Used with permission, GM Media Archives

1959

Rising Sun

TOYOTA ESCHEWED THE FASHION OF RACY-LOOKING MODELS by draping a beautiful woman in a traditional silk kimono at the 1959 Chicago Auto Show. The introduction was low key: It would take another 10 years before Toyota vehicles caught on with the public … and then sales skyrocketed. The rise of Toyota has been meteoric. Spending more than a million dollars per day on research, the company continues to bring products to market that the public did not know they wanted until they saw and experienced them. Examples would be the creation of their luxury brand, Lexus; their youth market brand, Scion; and the industry-leading hybrid vehicle, Prius.

PHOTO: Chicago Automobile Trade Association

1960

A Bevy of Beauties

AMERICA LOVES A PRETTY GIRL. And auto shows attracted beauty queens as representatives of the auto companies. Miss America could anticipate a sponsorship contract to appear for ribbon-cutting ceremonies. Beauty queens helped cement the understanding of a specific vehicle: Miss Hot Tamale from a chili festival, for example, could extol the power of "hot" engines. Top auto executives now took part in the selection of talent for the shows along with specific wardrobes.

In the picture at right, taken in the early 1960s, the Detroit Auto Dealers Association posed a group of auto show models before the show doors opened. The models each depicted a specific visual quality to enhance the car they were assigned to represent. The wardrobe ranged from Audrey Hepburn contemporary to Western cowgirl, New York sophisticate, Betty Crocker homemaker, and Marilyn Monroe lookalike.

PHOTO: National Automotive History Collection at Detroit Public Library

1960

Tale of the Comet

AN EARLY ENTRY into the compact class of cars for budget-minded consumers—the Comet—arrives in 1960 with four-part harmony. Here, auto show entertainment downsizes from a full-scale production to a small act at the show booth to draw patrons directly to the product. The Comet was originally referred to as the Edsel B—it was designed to be a compact car in the Edsel product line—but it received the "Mercury" moniker when Ford discontinued Edsel. It was based on the Ford Falcon platform. According to *Automotive News,* sales of U.S. cars and trucks had dipped to 7.2 million units in 1960. Sales of the new compact brands helped boost that figure to 10.5 million units by 1965.

PHOTO: National Automotive History Collection at Detroit Public Library

1960

Paradise of Pulchritude

CHARLES SNITOW, organizer of the New York Auto Show during the 1960s, referred to the abundance of models gracing the cars as the "Paradise of Pulchritude." To help the Detroit Auto Dealers Association promote its annual show at the newly built Cobo Hall in 1960, the group created a "Wheels of Freedom" float in the likeness of the hall, with women perched on top like toy dolls on a birthday cake. The 1960 Detroit Auto Show was the one time President Eisenhower visited Detroit. Today, Cobo Hall is the location of the North American International Auto Show held each January. Journalists and automakers from around the world gather to attend and present press conferences touting the newest vehicles and automotive information.

PHOTO: National Automotive History Collection at Detroit Public Library

1960

Risqué Business

A MODEL WEARS A NUDE-COLORED SWIMSUIT for a skit with an Emmett Kelly–inspired hobo to promote Chrysler at the 1960 Detroit Auto Show. Glenn Campbell, public relations director of the ad agency BBDO during the 1960s and 1970s and chief blogger for the *autowriters.com* newswire in the mid-2000s, said stark contrasts exist between the auto shows of the '60s and today. Earlier shows relied upon attractive models and hucksters to draw customers to the booth—the more entertaining, the better. Among the more daring was a human mannequin who dared people to make her blink, smile, or otherwise break her pose. In later years, Campbell noted, automakers would find talent to enhance—but never eclipse—the cars they represented.

PHOTO: National Automotive History Collection at Detroit Public Library

1960

More Leg Room

A LEGEND BECOMES A SIREN at the auto show. Marlene Dietrich, the German-born film star and chanteuse, whose signature song was "Falling in Love Again (Can't Help It)," had a perpetual love of fine cars. Her private collection spanned the great names in luxury classics of the era. Shown here at the 1960 Detroit Auto Show, Dietrich appeared in regal splendor endorsing a Mercedes seat concept. She added the allure of Hollywood glamour to the show in her mink coat and still-sensational legs.

PHOTO: National Automotive History Collection at Detroit Public Library

1960

Fashion Forward

GUCCI, BILL BLASS, Christian Dior, Oscar de la Renta, and others joined the auto design ranks. Designer vehicles created much media hype, and their designers also created signature outfits for live presenters. This elegant model, in a designer dress with dramatic cascading train, stands next to a 1960 Valiant station wagon. Although the dress may be more elegant than that of the everyday user of a station wagon, the model displayed an air of class and escape from the mundane for a suburban housewife who devoted most of her day to running errands in her "Mom Mobile."

PHOTO: National Automotive History Collection at Detroit Public Library

1961

Will the Real Gina Lollobrigida
Please Stand Up?

WHEN PONTIAC INTRODUCED THE TEMPEST MONTE CARLO show car at the 1961 Detroit Auto Show, three Italian models cast to resemble Hollywood's leading Mediterranean film star sported gold lamé jump suits and stiletto pumps. Although wardrobes are such pleasurable eye candy for the showgoer, they can create professional endurance trials for the models. Veteran auto show models refer to heavy chandelier earrings, ultra-tight waistlines and five-inch heels as the "price of looking glamorous" for a six- to eight-hour work shift. Despite the discomfort, true professional models manage to smile throughout their presentations.

PHOTO: Used with permission, GM Media Archives

1961

White-glove Inspection

TO CONVEY FASHION, BEAUTY, AND MOBILITY, this Doris Day lookalike poses in front of a cutaway seat and dashboard exhibit to demonstrate new interior design trends at the Chicago Auto Show in 1961. Notice the tiny platform on which she stands while wearing high-heeled pumps. One misstep and she could fall between the floor joists. Since then, exhibit builders and auto manufacturers have made significant ergonomic strides in how new cars and their components are presented to the public. The displays are always pushing the envelope to create an exciting and educational experience for consumers. Today's human models have remote devices to stop a revolving turntable if the heel of a shoe were to get caught. And the narrator's walking space is planned into the overall design.

1963

Live Bait

HOOD ORNAMENTS have adorned automobiles for decades, yet this sequin-gowned mermaid created a real-life version to mesmerize the multitudes at the Detroit Auto Show. She poses atop the new 1964 Plymouth Barracuda. Sirens with an irresistible song have dominated folklore for centuries, ever since Homer's ancient epic, *The Odyssey*, was first told around 800 B.C. Auto shows use real visual images to express the magical qualities of a car. The era of auto Sirens has created a bonding link between the promise of motoring excellence and personal ownership of a dream.

1965

Alice in the Land of Lure

BACK IN 1965, the New York World's Fair was the ultimate global automotive showcase of its day. For the fair, General Motors created a "Futurama" exhibit. Visitors rode into the future in concept vehicles moving through a series of exhibits. Attractive models added a sense of drama and interest to the look of approaching architecture and transportation trends. Here, taking a cue from "Alice in Wonderland," the heroine arranges toy pieces in an imaginary city inside GM's "Futurama" building, an estimated $8 million display. This "must see" display showed the power of the future to enchanted international fairgoers, which drew 29 million people during its two-year run.

PHOTO: National Automotive History Collection at Detroit Public Library

1966

Bad Kitty

NELL THEOBALD, the 21-year-old Miss BMW, looked fetching in lederhosen at a BMW press conference during the 1966 New York Auto Show. Seconds after this publicity photo was taken, with television cameras rolling, 225-pound Ludwig the Lion sunk his jaws into her thigh and held tight until his handlers could pry her loose. Doctors were able to save Theobald's leg, but post-traumatic stress interrupted her career.

According to a *New York Times* article that appeared in May 2006, after receiving $250,000 in damages from a subsequent lawsuit, Theobald became infatuated with the Swedish soprano, Birgit Nilsson, attending every one of her concerts around the world from 1968 to 1977. Theobald stalked Nilsson, even gaining access to her hotel rooms and backstage dressing rooms, stealing photos, dresses, and personal items. Nilsson's diary revealed that Theobald was a menacing presence in her life. Sadly, Theobald took her own life in 1977.

PHOTO: Used with permission, Corbis International

1966

Bumper Crop

THIS CUSTOM SHOW VERSION of the Dodge D100 "Sweptside" pickup truck was the preferred ride for a chrome-suited model with an oversize helmet at the 1966 Chicago Auto Show. Chrome first appeared on hood ornaments and grilles—especially in the 1930s. Shiny, metallic chrome plating—made of a thin deposit of chromium applied by an electrolytic process—also found widespread appeal in the 1950s and '60s.

Automotive historians speak fondly of "Dagmar" bumpers, particularly those chrome design elements found on 1950s Cadillacs, which paid homage to the bustline of the actress Dagmar. She was the bubble-headed blonde who appeared on the 1950 Jerry Lester TV show wearing low-cut gowns and conical brassieres.

PHOTO: Chicago Automobile Trade Association, Chicago Auto Show Collection

1967

Heroes and Villains

KICKING UP SALES IN THE MID-1960s, Dodge ran its famous "Dodge Girls" campaign. Casting agencies sought blondes with high-spirited personalities to become members of this nationally recognized group. They became the rock stars of their era at the auto shows. The campaign proved so popular that auto show patrons would swarm the stage for autographs, recalls Glenn Campbell, who was then public relations director of BBDO Advertising, which handled the Chrysler account. "Dodge Girls didn't dance on stage—instead we created a revolving platform for cars with women standing next to them," Campbell says. "That made it easier to train new girls along the show circuit." This advertisement, for the 1967 Dodge Coronet 440, speaks to a wilder, sexist era, according to Barry Dressel, director of the Walter P. Chrysler Museum in Auburn Hills, Michigan. "My comment," says Dressel, "is that I can't see how such a suggestive image could have been innocently produced."

ADVERTISEMENT: National Automotive History Collection at Detroit Public Library

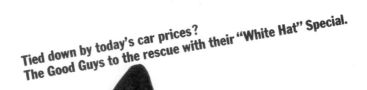

**Tied down by today's car prices?
The Good Guys to the rescue with their "White Hat" Special.**

What's a "White Hat" Special? It's a dazzling new Dodge Coronet 440—with the special features you have wanted at a special low package price! Listen to the list: your choice of a white or black vinyl top or a standard roof... deluxe wheel covers... white sidewall tires... bumper guards, front and rear... deluxe steering wheel... fender-mounted turn signals! Your choice of a 2-door hardtop (shown here) or a 4-door model! Colors? Choose again from a rainbow of nineteen! Air conditioning and V8 power? The Good Guys can make 'em yours for a breeze! Also, ask about the "White Hat" Special on Charger. Try a "White Hat" Special on for size. What more fitting way to join the Dodge Rebellion.

**The
Dodge
Rebellion
wants
you!**

Dodge   **CHRYSLER**
MOTORS CORPORATION

1967

Muscle Car Mania

RUNWAY MODELS LEND '60s SOPHISTICATION to the new Camaro, Chevrolet's 1967-model foray into the youth market. Often called the "pony" cars, they included the Ford Mustang, Plymouth Barracuda, Pontiac GTO, and AMC Javelin. The late John DeLorean, father of the Pontiac GTO and former vice president of General Motors, wrote the following insight on the youth car market with Patrick Wright in the book, *On a Clear Day You Can See General Motors*: "Capricious, energetic, and impressionable, America's young people have always been excited by cars. But their influence in car buying increased as the post-World War II economy grew, producing two-, three-, and even four-car families."

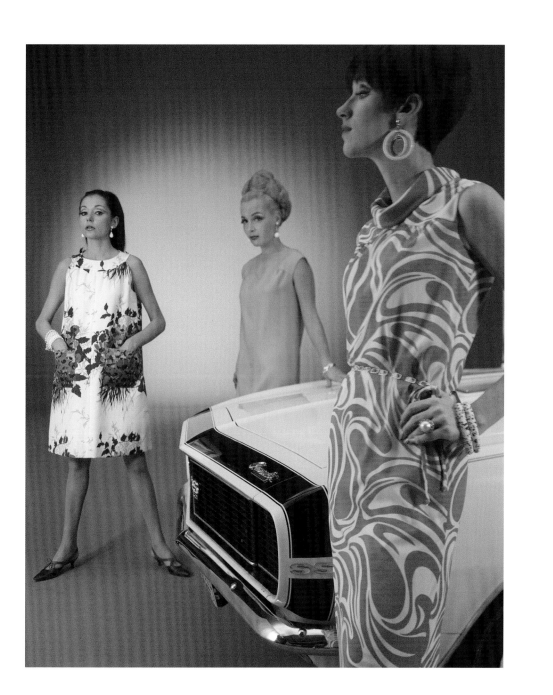

1969

Spectator Sport

A BLONDE MODEL in a mod, crocheted mini-dress captivated spectators at the New York International Auto Show in 1969, along with the Mercury Super Spoiler concept vehicle. Such sultry attire was a part of the show-business persona of auto shows. Models were used as attractions to the vehicles. For those occasions when they were perhaps too attractive, they had developed a system of communication, using signals and few words, to indicate that a patron was loitering a little too long at their work stations. Security guards were readily available to eject creepy individuals. Says one ex-auto show narrator: "If I had $10 for every guy who asked, 'Do you come with the car?' I could have retired a millionaire."

PHOTO: Bernie Weis

1969

Freedom of Mobility

THIS NEW YORK INTERNATIONAL AUTO SHOW poster from 1969, at the cusp of a new decade, speaks to the "wind-in-your-face" thrill of motoring. Ironically, this era also was about to usher in increased government involvement, with new safety, emissions, and fuel economy regulations. However, convertibles and a glamorous lifestyle were touted, along with music options and air conditioning. Now you could hit the open road in style. There were lots of things to see, hear, and touch at an auto show. Male models were hired as narrators and female counterparts gracefully showed how to open doors and check out the trunk.

POSTER: National Automotive History Collection at Detroit Public Library

INTERNATIONAL AUTOMOBILE SHOW NEW YORK COLISEUM

APRIL 5-13, 1969

official program

1969

Freeze Frame

"AUTOMOBILES ARE ALL ABOUT STATUS, SPEED, AND SEX," says Bill Rauhauser, former teacher at the Detroit School of Automotive Photography and co-author of *The Car and the Camera: The Detroit School of Automotive Photography* with David L. Lewis. In this photo, Rauhauser captures an artful model onstage with a 1969 Plymouth Sport Fury. An abundance of model and car photos available in the 1960s and '70s owe much to technical advances in photography and lighting. The automotive industry, auto shows, and auto advertising were a barometer of American culture, both mirroring and helping shape the spirit of the time.

PHOTO: Bill Rauhauser

1970

To Boldly Go Where No Woman Has Gone Before

TRADING ON THE POPULARITY OF THE 1960s *Star Trek* TV series, the first moon walk, and Isaac Asimov's science fiction novels, General Motors introduced a 1970 model Chevrolet Astro III concept vehicle. Orbited by a model in a futuristic jumpsuit, the high-performance vehicle was conceived for restricted-access highways. Mitchel J. Frumkin, co-author of *World's Greatest Auto Show*, noted that the vehicle has a tricycle-type wheel layout, a rear-mounted Allison gas turbine engine, and a rear-vision closed circuit TV, which might have alerted this driver to Klingon and Romulan vessels fast on her trail.

PHOTO: Bill Rauhauser

1971

Hell on Heels

MODELING WITH A 1971 PONTIAC GRAND VILLE four-door sedan in a designer gown, this model exudes poise and glamour. But the price of beauty in that era could be excruciating pain, according to Harriet Fuller, a top show model in the 1960s and '70s who co-founded Productions Plus, a talent agency with offices in Los Angeles, Chicago, and Detroit. Women in her modeling era stood in drafty exposition halls in sleeveless gowns with plunging necklines, unable to don a sweater lest it destroy the look. "We wore waist cinchers connected to a bra that pulled the stomach in and fastened in the back," Fuller recalls. "Our strapless bras pushed everything up—defying gravity— molding everything from the hipbones up for a flawless look. We wore our hair piled up, curls on top, held fast with Aqua Net hair spray. Add stage makeup, heather rouge to the face, and strappy pumps with very high heels. Your dress was so expensive you couldn't eat or drink in it. You took it off and put on a robe to eat your lunch."

PHOTO: Used with permission, GM Media Archives

1972

Models of Diversity

AN AFRICAN-AMERICAN MODEL graces the turntable with a 1972 Oldsmobile Contessa show car. Her presence on the circuit marked a greater interest in minority buyers and the expansion of multicultural events. This was an era of African-American superstars—from the sounds of Michael Jackson and Diana Ross to movies like *Shaft*. Voters elected black mayors in Detroit, Atlanta, and Los Angeles, and automotive dollars followed, with greater investments in multicultural markets.

PHOTO: Used with permission, GM Media Archives

1973

Three Jills, a Jack, and a Jag

THREE JAGUAR MODELS sport dresses that combine to form a Union Jack for a press conference at the 1973 New York International Auto Show. The sale of imported and domestic vehicles in the U.S. reached 13.9 million units that year, with spectacular shows, press conferences, and seductive models of all sorts contributing to the momentum. Leon Mandel, author of *American Cars,* speculated that the thrill and original demand for European and Asian cars came from veterans of global wars whose tastes and interests in products expanded beyond the U.S. border because of their overseas military service.

PHOTO: Bob Knoll

1973

From Russia with Fur

A MODEL IN A FUR BIKINI, cape, boots, and Cossack hat makes the Cold War seem a little warmer as she waves to crowds at the 1973 New York International Auto Show from atop a Soviet-built Lada UAZ 469 utility vehicle. According to historian Gregg Merksamer, customers said "nyet" to the Soviet jeep, but sales of prestige European imports such as Porsche, Mercedes, Volvo, BMW, and Saab experienced strong sales growth during this period.

PHOTO: Bernie Weis

DROP YOUR
NAME SUGGESTION
FOR THE SOVIET MADE
LADA
ALL-PURPOSE VEHICLE
IN OUR BOX

along with your
name and address

YOU MAY BE THE
LUCKY WINNER!

1975

The Model Who Would Be Heiress

IT'S NOT UNCOMMON FOR PRETTY WOMEN dressed in glamorous clothes to find love from the vantage point of a turntable. But the love story of Kathleen DuRoss and Henry Ford II was a modern-day fairy tale. Widowed with two children in the early 1960s, DuRoss went to night school to complete college and supported her family as a Ford Motor Co. auto show model. After some years on the circuit, she attracted the attention of Henry Ford II, then CEO of the auto company. DuRoss became part owner of L'Esprit, a disco in downtown Detroit, where Ford would meet her and dance with the town's glitterati. Their relationship became public in February 1975 when Ford was arrested on a highway near Santa Barbara, California, on drunken driving charges. DuRoss accompanied him. During the ensuing media frenzy, Ford made his famous remark: "Never complain, never explain." According to the *Detroit Free Press,* she married "The Deuce" in 1980 and enjoyed a storybook romance.

PHOTO: National Automotive History Collection at Detroit Public Library

1976

Working 'The Lean'

A MODEL STANDS NEXT TO the 1976 Cadillac Seville under bright lights of the New York Auto Show. She is working on "the basic lean"—a technique to show off the vehicle. This stance has been perfected by auto show models. The formula is to have one hand on the car, another hand on the hip, periodically leaning in and out. This tricky maneuver is more difficult than it sounds, as the model shown still needed both hands on the car for support. Henry Ford II personally gave instructions to his teams of models, stating: "You drape yourself over the car, and you act as though you love this vehicle. Periodically you can stand back, open the car door and pose as though about to sit in the car. But you never sit inside the car. Your body is always turned to the public looking fluid—not stiff."

PHOTO: Used with permission, GM Media Archives

1977

Pontiacs and Pantsuits

AUTOMAKERS OFTEN STATIONED GROUPS OF PRETTY WOMEN near the hot vehicles they wanted to market, such as this 1977 Formula edition of the fastback Pontiac Sunbird. Market research studies found show patrons wanted to see people on turntables wearing fashion trends that looked as up-to-the-minute as the latest concept cars. Impeccable grooming, great haircuts, perfect makeup, and fashion continued to take center stage.

PHOTO: Used with permission, GM Media Archives

1981

Living Doll

ADORNED BY A CROWN OF LIGHTS, a model adopts a Barbie pose while perched in a Pontiac Bonneville at the 1981 Chicago Auto Show. Barbie-like qualities are a powerful cultural symbol. When Barbie is placed next to just about anything, she gives it a new meaning. Trading on this lure has a legitimate business purpose: The car industry expects to sell new vehicles to at least one-third of the showgoers within six months of their attendance at an auto show.

PHOTO: Chicago Automobile Trade Association

1981

Sensible Suits

TWO WOMEN IN APPROPRIATE BUSINESS SUITS, popularized by then-popular fashion guru John Malloy, trumpet Buick's fuel efficiency measures to attendees of the 1981 Chicago Auto Show. In 1979, *Women's Day* magazine—in tandem with the National Automobile Dealers Association—released a study of new car-buying trends. It stated that 62 percent of the women who shopped with a man were "very influential" in the ultimate selection—50 percent more than auto dealers had believed. The women surveyed had less car-brand loyalty, opening a ripe market for pitching cars to women at auto shows. During the 1980s, car companies began to use focus groups made up of women employees who assessed vehicles for ease of entry, transporting children, and safety factors. A series of studies by *Family Circle* and *Cosmopolitan* magazines also helped modeling agencies such as Productions Plus lobby automotive marketing executives to revamp their wardrobes to address women consumers. Women buyers wanted professional narrators who looked and acted the lifestyle of the brand. By the 1990s, almost 90 percent of the show narrators had college degrees and used their smarts on the turntables during presentations.

PHOTO: Chicago Automobile Trade Association

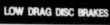

1982

Assembly Line Siren

AUTO SHOW MODEL ANITA MITZEL faced her toughest assignment in 1982—assembling and reassembling an engine block while telling the history of Cadillac. This job required total concentration and rhythm, as she had to lip-synch much of her script to a pre-recorded track. With more high-tech features being integrated into exhibits, models needed to keep current, using broadcaster skills to read a TelePrompTer, demonstrate a computer, host a game show, personify a technical adviser, or use American Sign Language.

Some auto companies treated models like stars during the shows, supplying them with a new automobile, a tank of gas, and free dinners. What did she eat? The model's diet: soup and dessert, or salad and dessert, or an appetizer and dessert. "You had to fit into your dress the next day," Mitzel said.

PHOTO: Courtesy of Anita Mitzel

1983

Flipping for Nissan

ALIGNING ITSELF WITH AMERICAN ATHLETES while showcasing lithe forms in fascinating movements, Nissan created a red, white, and blue gym on its stage during the 1983 Chicago Auto Show. That same year, it invested an estimated $30 million to change its name from Datsun to Nissan, and its advertising motto from "We are Driven" to "The Name is Nissan."

PHOTO: Chicago Automobile Association

1985

The Man-hood Ornament

A MODERN-DAY HERMES—GOD OF SPEED. *The Michigan Woman* magazine posed model Larry Weathers atop a red Chevrolet Corvette on its fall 1985 cover. The goal was to prompt controversy about the way women reacted to marketing that was geared to them. It asked if women sought sex symbols as bait for car sales.

By 2008, male models numbered 35 percent of the talent at the auto shows. Many of the men say women rarely make suggestive remarks, but smile with appreciation for a handsome face and rugged physique. Jonathon Bray, a Scion product specialist, actor, and Los Angeles resident, said: "Primarily, men come to shows with other guys or they come with their families or their dates. Shows aren't a destination for single women. I could wish."

COVER: Used with permission by *The Michigan Woman* editor Sue McDonald

Breaking out: Two women alcoholics tell their stories

THE MICHIGAN WOMAN

OCT./NOV. $1.95

Is this any way to sell cars to women?

SPECIAL SECTION
WOMEN AND CARS

1989

What Models See

CHICAGO AUTO SHOW PATRONS saw a product specialist in a swirling gown waxing eloquently about a 1989 Pontiac Grand Prix. But this perspective shows what a model might see as she looks out into the crowd. Talk to dozens of auto show models, and you will hear a familiar refrain:

"You see every type of person imaginable."

"You watch mothers take their babies into the back seat of an open vehicle to change diapers and dump the remains."

"Teenage couples sneak into cars to neck." (You can tell something torrid is happening because the windows fog up.)

"Gang members sneak in with an assignment to steal a cigarette lighter or hood ornament."

"Some people act rude to try and get you to yell at them."

So what makes the job fun? "You get marriage proposals all the time. The men say their wives don't understand cars half as well as I do."

PHOTO: Chicago Automobile Trade Association

152

1990

Geo Global

CHEVROLET INTRODUCED THE 1990 GEO STORM at the Chicago Auto Show with fast-dancing females to showcase the low-priced model built in Japan by Isuzu. Hot music and dance—a reinstated element at the shows—added an entertainment factor that drew big crowds.

Often, product spokespeople representing Japanese brands had to deal with patrons who were angry at them for promoting non-U.S. companies. The spokespeople would politely attempt to educate consumers on the global nature of the evolving auto business and the growing number of transplants and U.S. jobs created by these automakers.

PHOTO: Chicago Automobile Trade Association

1990

Men at Work

A NEW BREED OF AUTO SHOW TALENT joined the exhibits when teams of actual United Auto Workers demonstrated production techniques and explained how cars were made. This photo shows the Buick Reatta team at the 1990 North American International Auto Show in Detroit. This touch of reality dispensed by men and women who actually worked on the assembly line was used by many manufacturers—including Toyota, Nissan, and Honda.

More men have become product spokespeople and narrators on turntables around the show floor. People still tended to look to the men to answer product questions even when they were standing next to a female counterpart.

PHOTO: National Automobile History Collection at Detroit Public Library

1992

Raising Standards

MARGERY KREVSKY (right) and Harriet Fuller (left) started Productions Plus in 1981, redefining the role of auto show models. Today the agency's scope is international. Highly technical cars and fierce competition prompted automakers to enlist agencies such as Productions Plus to train, wardrobe, and manage the voice and spirit of their respective brands. Now called "Product Specialists," the talent need strong credentials to work the auto show floor:

- A degree in communications, engineering, theater, or business.
- Travel the U.S. to learn the buying specifics of each geographical area.
- Presentation and improv skills to impart information and judge what the audience wants to know.
- Ability to "talk car" and mastery of Automotive 101.
- Concentrated training sessions on the vehicle lineup.

> "Yes, auto shows can be fun and entertaining for the showgoer, but they are also a fiercely competitive battleground where millions of dollars are spent by some of the world's biggest brands."
>
> — Joe Gallant, Manager, Shows and Exhibits, Nissan North America

PHOTO: Glenn Triest

1998

The Great Reveal

EXCITEMENT REACHES A CRESCENDO at press conferences when attractive models, such as these four Mitsubishi SST models at the Chicago Auto Show in 1998, take the wraps off a new offering. Camera shutters snap, reporters scribble, and TV cameras record it for the nightly news. Nearly every large city hosts two or three days of press conferences with increasing degrees of theatrical excitement to capture the attention of journalists—anywhere from 4,000 to 8,000 journalists attend the top four shows in Chicago, Detroit, Los Angeles, and New York City. Such attention fires passion for the public show days, and global telecasts whet car-lovers' appetites around the world.

PHOTO: Chicago Automobile Trade Association

2003

Diva Does Detroit

INTERNATIONAL SONGSTRESS CELINE DION headlined the DaimlerChrysler booth at the Charity Preview of the 2003 North American International Auto Show in Detroit. Her brilliant star power even outshone the cars. It was a magic night for the auto industry with people purchasing charity preview tickets for more than $300 each. Tickets sold out months in advance, and last-minute attendees scrambled to get their hands on tickets even if it meant paying a premium. Automakers exercise care to find personalities who can enhance the brand.

> "Auto shows are 'events' founded and built on passion. A visitor can be an enthusiast or simply a dreamer drawn to what 'can be.'"

> — Rod Alberts, Executive Director, North American International Auto Show

PHOTO: Len Katz, Courtesy of Detroit Auto Dealers Association

2005

Practice Makes Perfect

BEFORE THE LEXUS PRODUCT SPECIALISTS take to their turntables and vehicle stands, they spend time reviewing the latest product literature, manufacturing updates, and events. Each narration lasts around five minutes, communicating only the essential points. About 40 percent of show patrons are really serious about buying a vehicle in the next six months, according to Lexus research. The 20 million people who see shows in the 85 cities where Lexus has a presence pay to get in the door and learn more about cars. A good presentation can help consumers narrow their search from a convention center full of sheet metal down to one or two vehicles. How do product spokespeople remember their scripts? Many are trained to use a mnemonic device called "SPACED" to make sure they have covered all the bases in their five-minute talk. SPACED stands for Safety, Performance, Appearance, Comfort and convenience, Easy to own, and Durability.

PHOTO: Jerome Magid

2005

Zwei for the Road

A BRIGHT GOLDEN CONCEPT CAR FROM CZECH AUTOMAKER ŠKODA took center stage in Frankfurt. But the Volkswagen Group subsidiary's offering may have been overshadowed by two fräuleins in hot pants flashing sultry looks. The Frankfurt show originated in 1897 with a mini exhibition in a Berlin hotel, and was called the Internationale Automobil-Ausstellung (IAA). From 1921–'26, no international exhibitors were allowed because of the aftermath of World War I. The show moved permanently to Frankfurt in 1951.

As you might expect the Frankfurt show is dominated by German manufacturers. Companies like Audi, BMW, Mercedes-Benz, and Porsche typically use the show as their launching pad for new models. It's still an international show, however, with brands from around the world. If there's one thing that distinguishes this show from others it is the sheer size. Spreading out over 10 halls you will get quite a workout walking several miles. BMW and Mercedes have created halls of their very own, giving you an up-close and personal brand experience.

PHOTO: Productions Plus

2005

Meet the Jetsons

MAKING A SOCIAL AND FASHION STATEMENT, Toyota showed its i-unit at the 2005 New York Auto Show. Designed by Yoshiaki Kato, it was an upright vehicle designed to move among people at low speed. It reclined to lower the center of gravity for higher speeds. The driver support information used sound, light, and vibration to communicate, and its body color would be personalized according to the driver's preferences and emotions. Product Specialist Wende Gustafson sports a white ensemble with an iridescent silver collar that looks like it might have been inspired by the '60s TV show, *The Jetsons*.

PHOTO: Productions Plus

2005

Fiat Friends

MODELS FOR ITALIAN AUTOMAKER FIAT—shown at the 2005 Frankfurt Auto Show in Germany—are dressed in jeans and a very identifiably branded casual jacket to portray a lifestyle: young and hip, with an affordable car. Marketing toward the youth segment is seen as the lifeblood for the future of auto manufacturers.

The Frankfurt show is a biennial event, alternating with the Paris Motor Show. The well-attended show brings to light many of the newest and most creative designs. German manufacturers particularly invest in major exhibits, often creating their own buildings on the exhibit grounds to showcase their vehicles.

PHOTO: Productions Plus

2005

Handle With Care

"CARS ARE FRAGILE WITHOUT ESP" is spelled out on the wardrobe of models at the 2005 Frankfurt Auto Show. Additionally, temporary tattoos on the models' bodies spell out the words "FRAGILE." The models were at the German auto supplier Bosch's technology booth promoting its Electronic Stability Program (ESP)—a technology that detects and counteracts skidding.

PHOTO: Productions Plus

2006

Les Femmes

TWO FRENCH MODELS POSE FOR PHOTOGRAPHERS in an Alfa Romeo during press days before the public opening of the 2006 Mondial de l'Automobile (Paris Motor Show). The show is held every other year in the fall and features concept car debuts and new production technology. It was the first motor show in the world—started in 1898 by industry pioneer Albert de Dion. Only a handful of the newfangled "automobiles" were exhibited at the first show. To prove the validity of this new mode of transportation, exhibitors had to drive their vehicles from Versailles to Paris. Over the years many incredible cars have made their debuts in Paris, including Porsche's 605-horsepower Carrera GT supercar, Bentley's Continental GT, and Ferrari's $670,000 Enzo.

PHOTO: Productions Plus

2006

'Have You Seen the Lancia Girls?'

THAT WAS THE BUZZ ON THE FLOOR of the 2006 Paris Motor Show. One element of the Paris Motor Show is the extensive use of designer couture and beautiful women. Italian automaker Lancia succeeded—the exhibit was swamped with photographers and executives from many of the other exhibits. The cascading necklacesand chic cocktail dresses exemplify a luxurious Parisian persona. At today's Paris show, sirens are professional models true to the French spirit—they combine allure, glamour, couture, and the ability to smile all day. They may not know much about the nuts and bolts of automobiles, but their style and charm create a trés Parisian dynamic.

PHOTO: Productions Plus

2007

Win on Sunday, Sell on Monday

COLOMBIAN FORMULA ONE RACER TURNED NASCAR star Juan Carlos Montoya shakes hands with Chrysler COO Eric Ridenour at a press conference for the Dodge Avenger during the 2007 North American International Auto Show in Detroit. Racing stars have generated allure for automobiles since the earliest days of the industry, when pioneers such as Barney Oldfield raced for Ford Motor Company, and Louis Chevrolet raced for what would later become General Motors. In the 21st century, the term "NASCAR dad" signified a potent economic and political force of middle-class men who loved watching fast cars live at racetracks and on wide-screen television sets.

PHOTO: Courtesy of the Detroit Auto Dealers Association

2007

Made for Each Other

FASHION AND FOUR WHEELS have remained a staple of auto show society for better than 100 years. These chrome cocktail dresses were designed by Nora del Busto, a student at the International Academy of Design and Technology, for the GM International Academy of Design and Technology Fashion Show at Chicago's Union Station in 2007. The muses were the 2008 Buick Enclave (top right) and the Chevrolet Volt electric concept car. Wardrobes for models and product specialists are designed specifically to "work" with the car. Both the designs and the car have similar details in their styling, or they match a color. Auto manufacturers have specific colors that are solely identifiable to their brands. In a throwback to the '60s, fashion shows are staged in the largest cities as a way to draw a diverse, hip, and fashion-forward crowd to American cars. Models represent multiple languages and global hues—much as the vehicles and their countries of origin.

PHOTOS: Mitchel J. Frumkin

2007

The Shanghai Swing

WITH A HIP-HOPPING ECONOMY and a yen for fast wheels, the exhibitors at the Shanghai Auto Show pulled out the stops in 2007, helping dance in annual car sales of 5.2 million that year in China, according to *Automotive News Europe*. Dancers gyrating to blasting Asian music introduced the NCV, a vehicle produced by Huanghai Auto. While the car glittered as much as the models, the auto press from NextAutos.com and others accused Huanghai of fusing borrowed designs from the Pontiac Torrent and the Lexus RX350. The controversy over branding only helped escalate show crowds—some 500,000 came to also see the Cherry, Chang Feng, Brilliance, and other emerging brands.

PHOTO: Roger Hart, managing editor of AutoWeek in Detroit

1938
A model in a Roman-inspired dress and winged tiara perches atop a "sharknose" Graham at the National Automobile Show in New York's Central Palace.

PHOTO
National Automotive History Collection at Detroit Public Library

SOURCES

SOURCES FOR QUOTATIONS AND VALIDATION HAVE BEEN MANY AND VARIED. HERE IS A LISTING OF BOOKS, ARTICLES, AND RESEARCH THAT INSPIRED NEW IDEAS OR FOSTERED QUOTATIONS FOR *SIRENS OF CHROME*:

20th Century Pop Culture,
by Dan Epstein,
Carlton Books Unlimited
(1999).

*A History of the New York
International Auto Show,
1900-2000,*
by Gregg D. Merksamer,
Lionheart Books (2000).

*A Look at Detroit, Auto Show
Images of the 1970s,*
by Bill Rauhauser,
LittleBeast, an imprint of
Press Lorentz (2007).

American Cars,
by Leon Mandel, Stewart,
Tabori & Chang (1982).

Automobiles of America,
by the Automobile
Manufacturers Association, Inc.,
(a) Savoyard Book, Wayne State
University Press (1970).

*Automotive News,
100 Events That Made the
Industry: Centennial Edition,
1896-1996,*
Crain Communications
(June 26, 1996).

Car Hops and Curb Service:
*A History of American Drive-in
Restaurants 1920-1960,*
by Jim Heimann,
Chronicle Books (1996).

Confessions of a Fast Woman,
by Lesley Hazelton,
Addison-Wesley Publishing
Company Inc. (1992).

*Driven: The American
Four-Wheeled Love Affair,*
Stein and Day (1977).

*On a Clear Day You
Can See General Motors:
John Z. DeLorean's Look Inside
the Automotive Giant,*
Wright Enterprises (1979).

*Only Yesterday:
An Informal History of the 1920s,*
by Frederick Lewis Allen,
Harper and Brothers (1931).

Sirens: Symbols of Seduction,
by Meri Lao,
Park Street Press (1998).

*The American Automobile:
A Centenary, 1893-1993,*
by Nick Georgano,
Prion/Smithmark (1993).

*The Automobile and
American Culture,*
an anthology assembled
by David L. Lewis and
Laurence Goldstein,
University of Michigan
Press (1980).

*The Car and the Camera:
The Detroit School of
Automotive Photography,*
by David Lewis and Bill
Rauhauser,
Wayne State University
Press (1996).

*The End of Detroit:
How the Big Three Lost Their Grip
on the America Car Market,*
by Micheline Maynard,
Currency Doubleday (2003).

*The Ford Century: Ford Motor
Company and the Innovations that
Shaped the World,*
by Russ Banham,
Artisan Books (2002).

*The First Century of the Detroit
Auto Show,*
by Robert Szudarek,
Society of Automotive
Engineers (2000).

*The GM Motorama:
Dream Cars of the Fifties,*
by Bruce Berghoff,
Motor Books
International (1995).

*The Song of Eve: An Illustrated
Journey into the Myths, Symbols
and Rituals of the Goddess,*
by Manuaela Dunn Mascetti,
Simon and Schuster Inc. (1990).

*The Story of the
American Automobile,*
by Rudolph E. Anderson,
Public Affairs Press (1950).

Those Wonderful Old Automobiles,
by Floyd Clymer,
Bonanza Books (1953).

*World's Greatest Auto Show,
Celebrating a Century in Chicago,*
by James M. Flammang and
Mitchel J. Frumkin,
Krause Publications (1998).

DO YOU COME WITH THE CAR?

NARRATORS SPEAK OUT AT THE NEW YORK INTERNATIONAL AUTO SHOW

by CAROL LAY

CATHY FEIL EXPLAINED WHY CAR-SHOW MODELS ARE NOW CALLED NARRATORS.

WE'RE VERY KNOWLEDGE-ABLE, MORE CLASSY, MORE ELEGANT — NOT JUST SEX SYMBOLS LYING ON CARS.

TRICIA SOSINSKI WAS IN THE MIDDLE OF A PRESENTATION WHEN...

I GOT A TERRIBLE CASE OF THE HICCUPS!

IT DREW A CROWD!

KIM WILLETT IS THE FIRST SIGN-LANGUAGE INTERPRETER TO DO PRESENTATION.

AIRBAG

YOU HAVE TO SPELL IT OUT FIRST.

RECENTLY, RENEÉ GODIN ACCIDENTALLY SLAMMED HER FINGER IN THE DOOR OF A CONCEPT CAR THAT HAS NO HANDLES.

THE CAR HAS A VOICE-OPERATED OPENING SYSTEM, BUT ONCE MY FINGER WAS CAUGHT MY VOICE CHANGED. IT WAS NO LONGER "OPEN" — IT WAS, LIKE, ♫OPEN♪

IT WAS THE LONGEST TEN SECONDS OF MY LIFE!

JANET POUND HAS BEEN ON THE CIRCUIT FOR FIVE YEARS.

WE'RE LIKE TRAVELLING GYPSIES, BUT MOST OF US HAVE ALL OUR TEETH.

AND THAD AVERY THINKS THE FEMALE NARRATORS GET MORE ATTENTION.

I WOULD LOVE TO HAVE SOME GIRLS OGLE ME, BUT SO FAR IT'S JUST BEEN VERY ATTENTIVE GENTLEMEN.

DO YOU COME WITH THE CAR?

1994
New Yorker magazine sent illustrator Carol Lay to the New York International Auto Show to capture the careers of car models. Her result is more truth than caricature.

ILLUSTRATION
Courtesy of Carol Lay

ACKNOWLEDGEMENTS

AS I'VE TRAVELED COAST TO COAST managing legions of talented individuals who perform at auto shows, I've gained enormous respect for their professionalism. I dedicate this book to each and every person who has worked shows for Productions Plus and other agencies.

This book is also dedicated to my husband, Seymour Krevsky, who has endured many evening hours alone so I could attend auto shows and compile this collection.

I also wish to thank the efforts of my management team at Productions Plus who gave me the time and support to focus on creating this homage to auto shows.

I would like to thank my ghost writer and researcher, Maureen McDonald, for the vast amount of work and effort she spent finding photographs, interviewing car buffs, sifting through historical books, and making it all come together. Her mind and energy kept our project alive while I was focused on running a company. Her spirit, humor, and willingness were a necessary part to make this book happen. Her research was aided by the countless hours Mark Patrick and Barbara Thompson of the National Automotive History Collection at the Detroit Public Library devoted to the task. Patricia Watkins and Gretchen Van Monette helped with research and coordination. Michael W.R. Davis, author of several automotive books, served as coach and mentor. Paul Grodin and Jer Patryjak provided invaluable assistance in understanding the exhibits side of auto shows.

Gregg D. Merksamer, author of *A History of the New York International Auto Show,* contributed photographs and behind-the-scenes stories; Mitchel J. Frumkin, co-author of *World's Greatest Auto Show: Celebrating a Century in Chicago,* found a treasure-trove of archival photos. The photo departments of General Motors and Ford were helpful, as were the archivists at Chrysler. The collections of several other authors, photo agencies, photographers, and more added to the lively mix.

I'd also like to thank the team at Momentum Books for bringing this concept to life. My hope is that readers will enjoy and understand more about the lives of the *Sirens of Chrome*—the beautiful, alluring people whose names are largely unknown, but whose contributions are part of our love affair with the automobile.

— Margery Krevsky

Don Sommer, founder of the Meadow Brook Concours d'Elegance in Rochester Hills, Michigan, produces fanciful replicas of classic hood ornaments in silvery perfection.

(1) 1925–'28:
Diana, mascot of the Diana Motors Co. of St. Louis, inspired by a sculpture by Anna Hyatt Huntington.

(2) 1932–'37:
Packard "Goddess of Speed," designed by Werner H.A. Gublitz and given the sobriquet of "Donut Chaser" by car collectors.

(3) 1930–'32:
Cadillac "Goddess," a streamlined Art Deco design by C.J. Klein and J.R. Morgan.

(4) 1933–'36:
Cadillac "Goddess II," designed by William Schnell.

PHOTOS
Courtesy of Don Sommer, Meadow Brook Concours d'Elegance

1

2

3

4

INDEX

INDEX

INDEX

INDEX